WITHDRAWN

How to Draw

Christmas
Things

For Jesse, Jasmine, Justin, Jordan, Melina, and Matthew

Published in the United States of America by The Child's World®
PO Box 326 • Chanhassen, MN 55317-0326
800-599-READ • www.childsworld.com

Acknowledgments
Illustration and Design: Rob Court
Production: The Creative Spark, San Juan Capistrano, CA

Library of Congress Cataloging-in-Publication Data
Court, Rob, 1956–
  How to draw Christmas things / by Rob Court.
     p. cm. — (Doodle books)
  ISBN-13: 978-1-59296-805-3 (library bound : alk. paper)
  ISBN-10: 1-59296-805-8 (library bound : alk. paper)
  1. Christmas in art—Juvenile literature. 2. Drawing—Technique—Juvenile
literature. I. Title. II. Series.

NC825.C49C68 2007
743'.893942663—dc22
                                        2006031559

The Scribbles Institute™

Doodle BOOKS ™

How to Draw

Christmas
Things

by Rob Court

The Child's World®

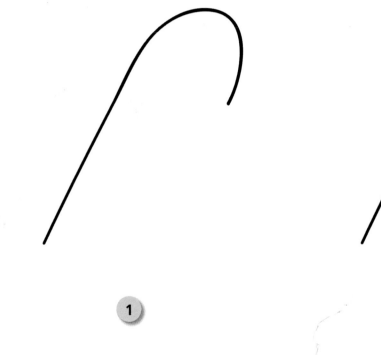

1

2

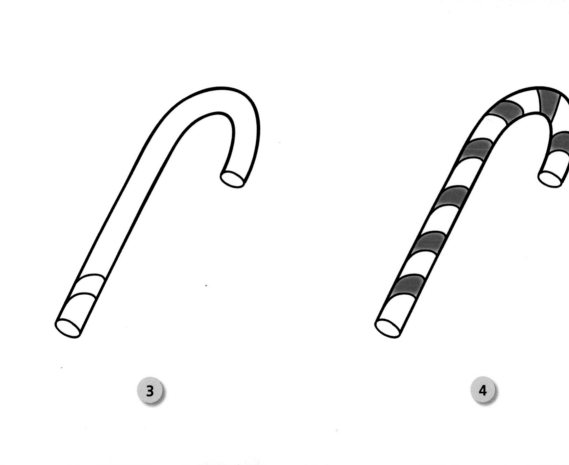

3

4

reindeer

1

2

3

4

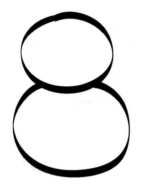

1

2

3

4

1

2

3

4

1

2

3

4

Christmas tree

1

2

3

4

sleigh

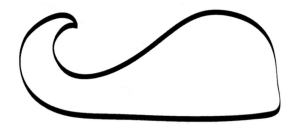

1

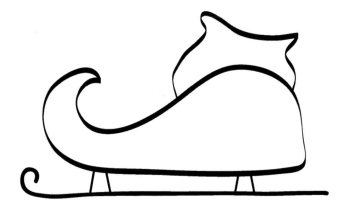

2

3

4

wreath

1

2

3

4

1

2

3

4

1

2

3

4

gift

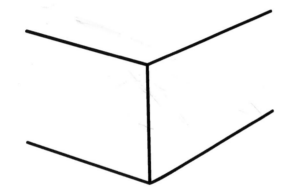

1

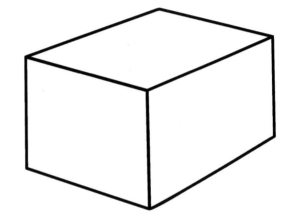

2

3

4

angel

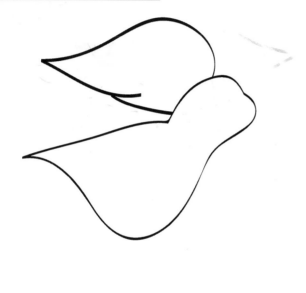

1

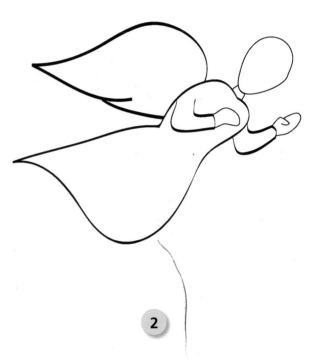

2

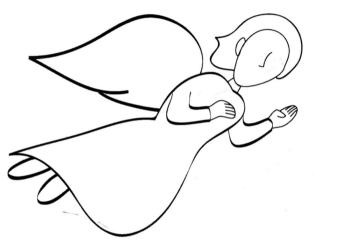

3

4

1

2

3

4

Santa Claus

1

2

3

4

lines

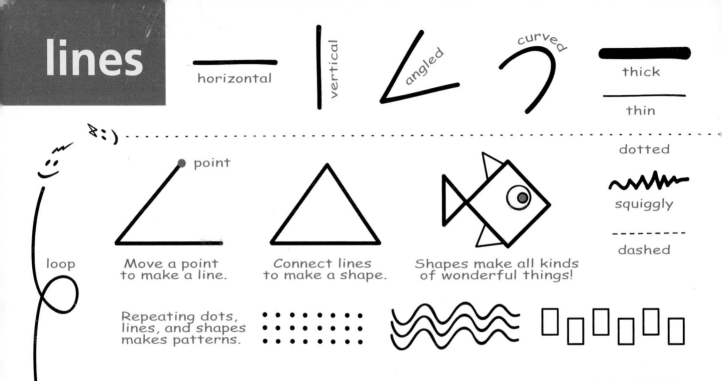

horizontal

vertical

angled

curved

thick

thin

dotted

point

squiggly

dashed

loop

Move a point to make a line.

Connect lines to make a shape.

Shapes make all kinds of wonderful things!

Repeating dots, lines, and shapes makes patterns.

About the Author

Rob Court is a graphic artist and illustrator. He started the Scribbles Institute to help students, parents, and teachers learn about drawing and visual art. Please visit www.scribblesinstitute.com